GW00739117

Serve a Liberal Helping

edited by Louise Malin

**Front cover
Nick Wadley**

Published by Camden Liberal Democrats

To order more copies email cookbook@camdenlibdems.org.uk
or visit www.camdenlibdems.org.uk/cookbook

ISBN 0 987-0-9556331-0-2

Copyright © 2007 Camden Liberal Democrats

CONTENTS

FOREWORD

It is always enjoyable to meet up with friends and share good food. So when Louise Malin suggested reaching out to our friends in the Liberal Democrats – both here in Camden and across the country – to compile this recipe book, I thought it was an excellent idea. We cannot always be fortunate enough to dine with such illustrious companions as Sir Clement Freud, Dame Shirley Williams, Sir Menzies Campbell or Camden's own Flick Rea, whose annual Christmas parties are the stuff of culinary legend. But by sharing their recipes, we can at least bring a little of their character to our tables.

On behalf of Camden Liberal Democrats, I would like to thank all the contributors for their willing co-operation, and apologise for any mistakes or omissions. Each recipe has been provided voluntarily, and we have done our best where necessary to obtain permission to reproduce them.

To our readers, I would like to pass on the sound advice of Andrew Arbuckle MSP, that 'anyone not wishing to cook for themselves cultivates a wide range of friends who can cook.' Whilst we have taken great care to transcribe the recipes as provided, they have not been tested and we cannot guarantee perfect results every time. Some recipes may contain nuts, raw eggs, alcohol or other ingredients that are subject to the usual health warnings. When reheating, always ensure food is served piping hot.

Finally, I would like to pay tribute to the army of volunteers without whom this project – and indeed so much of what we undertake in the Liberal Democrats – would never have been possible. In particular we are indebted to Louise Malin for her enthusiasm, hard work and perseverance in first of all conceiving the idea and then seeing it through to completion.

Please take time to enjoy these recipes and, above all, have fun.

Phil Wainewright
Chair, Camden Liberal Democrats

Wine and Food:
The Liberal Approach
By Robin Young

Wine and food is a natural partnership, yet to read many commentators you might think pairing the two is an obstacle course beset with traps and pitfalls.

So let me urge readers of this liberally inspired cookbook to adopt a wholeheartedly enlightened, liberal and democratic attitude to their choice of wines, and not to allow their full enjoyment to be restrained by ancient myths and unsoundly based rules and regulations.

Take (and immediately discard) for example the most oft-quoted of rules — red with meat and white with fish. It is rubbish. In wine-producing countries there is no shortage of recipes for fish cooked in red wine. Many people find young, fresh and fruity red wines (probably served chilled, thus breaking a second outmoded rule that reds are served at room temperature) as delightful with any fish dishes as white.

Let stuffy conservatives and champagne socialists monopolise authoritarian diktats. Liberals never fear to innovate, to experiment or make rational application of the most up-to-date knowledge.

So let the rancorous reactionaries and retrogressives grumble about modern advances in wine technology and wine commentary, while we liberals revel and glory in the added hedonistic pleasures they can bring.

A common complaint from the tut-tutting traditionalists is that modern wine writers are over-fanciful in their language. The old school say, "A wine is not appley or blackcurranty. It does not taste of raspberries, cherries or strawberries. It just tastes and smells of wine."

Simplistic — and regrettably wrong.

Modern wine writers often use improbable-seeming words such as green pepper to describe a selection of Cabernet Sauvignon wines, or banana to epitomise Beaujolais Nouveau. Yet in both instances, and many others, wine research laboratories have shown that the same aromatic chemical compounds are actually shared between the wine and the fruit with which it is compared.

So don't mock or denigrate the

"let me urge readers of this liberally inspired cookbook to adopt a wholeheartedly enlightened, liberal and democratic attitude to their choice of wines,"

assistance that back labels and wine writers offer, when they attempt to explain what your wine will taste like.

When, for example, wine writers say many white wines made from Chardonnay grapes have "buttery" texture they are in fact telling you that such wine will go with dishes you might want to accompany with a buttery sauce. That would include, for example, salmon, turbot or asparagus, but also grilled steak or chops.

Cabernet sauvignon is commonly described as having blackcurrant flavour, cabernet franc redcurrant, merlot is plummy, tannat raspberry perfumed, zinfandel blackberry-like, and top Italian chianti can taste like a bowl of cherries. Among whites chenin blanc is most often appley, sauvignon blanc gooseberryish (and so good with such diverse dishes as cream cheeses, grilled mackerel or fish and chips).

Matching wines with food then, should become an exercise rather like matching sauces and jellies or herbs and spices to meals. Do you prefer mint or redcurrant jelly with lamb, insist on apple sauce with pork, or like lemon on your fish or chicken? The wines are available to match whatever your preference may be.

So don't disregard wine commentators' wine descriptions as hopelessly fanciful, but equally never fear to seek out or invent matches of your own which you particularly enjoy. After that only one liberal principle remains to be observed: do whatever you like in matching wine with food but do not impose your more peculiarly personal preferences too autocratically on others, whose tastes might be quite different. The harm principle enunciated by that founding father of liberalism, John Stuart Mill, applies to wine as it does to anything else: feel free to do what you want, as long as it is not injurious. Excess is out, but be bold — enjoy !

STARTERS

Billybi

Sir Clement Freud

INGREDIENTS:

1 pint of mussels

1 ½ glasses dry white wine

2 glasses of water

A dozen crushed peppercorns

A few parsley stalks

A twist of lemon peel

1 oz sliced onion

METHOD:

Wash and scrape the mussels.

Put the ingredients into a large pan and bring to the boil over a strong flame.

When mussels have opened, turn down the flame and let them simmer for a few minutes to flavour the liquid.

Strain off the liquid and reduce by about a quarter by boiling.

TO THICKEN SOUP

1 oz butter

1 oz plain flour

¼ pint single cream

¼ pint double cream

When the soup is thus reduced, add the beurre manie (flour rubbed into butter), whisk as it simmers, and as it thickens add the cream.

Season to taste and serve very hot.

SIR CLEMENT WRITES...

This can be spelt many other ways. It is a soup that started life in oyster restaurants where the main ingredient was the contents of the bucket under the oysterman's feet, containing the beards and juice of a couple of hundred oysters. The juice of mussels, clams or scallops gives just as satisfactory a result or tinned clams which can be liquidized and passed through a sieve. It is essentially a by-product soup, but well worth creating for its own sake.

With kind permission 'Freud on Food' published in the 1970's

Courgette and Cumin Soup

David Heath CBE MP, Somerton and Frome

INGREDIENTS:

1 oz butter	5oz potato
1 onion	¾ pint of vegetable stock
1 clove of garlic	½ pint of milk
1 tps cumin	Salt and pepper to taste
12oz courgettes	

METHOD:

Fry the chopped onions and garlic in the butter for 5 minutes until soft.
Add the sliced courgettes, diced potato and cumin, cook for 2 minutes.
Add stock and milk.
Simmer approximately for 15 minutes until vegetables are soft.
Cool slightly, puree and season to taste.

Serve with warm crusty bread.

DAVID WRITES...

My wife's mother used to make this soup, it's easy, delicious and is a great way of using up the glut of courgettes we get from the garden in the summer.

Grav'Lax

Serves 8

Peter Mair, Camden Liberal Democrat

INGREDIENTS:

1.35kg fresh salmon (either a
whole fish or a piece)
4 tbls of salt
4 tbls caster sugar
2 tsp peppercorns, crushed

2 tsp corn oil
Lots of dill, both fronds and
stalks (ie 2 very large bunches
from a greengrocer)

METHOD:

Get your fishmonger to de-scale the salmon (important this, as otherwise
the scales will get everywhere, including into the finished dish), then fillet it
lengthways taking out the spine and removing head and tail, if applicable.
Mix the salt, sugar and pepper. Moisten the flesh side of each fillet with the
oil and rub with the salt, sugar, pepper mixture.
Lay a thick layer of dill in a dish with a lid, big enough to take the fish flat.
Lay one fillet on the dill skin side down.
Place another layer of dill on the flesh of this first fillet.
Place the second fillet, flesh side down and head to tail, on the dill.
Place yet more dill over the top. If possible, place grease proof paper on
the whole fish and weight it down. Place the container, with its lid on, in the
fridge for 72 hours, turning over the whole lot, fish and dill, every 12 hours.

TO SERVE

Discard the dill. Wipe the salt, sugar, pepper mix, and the oil, off the fish,
then slice the flesh thinly with your sharpest knife.
Swedes serve Grav'lax with rye bread and mustard sauce. I like German
pumpernickel bread with this dish.

PETER WRITES...

Grav'lax or gravadlax means literally "buried salmon" in Swedish.
Traditionally salmon was preserved by burying it, wrapped in dill. It could
be dug up for consumption at a later date. Clearly a lot of dill would
be needed as a preservative, and this is the secret of making Gravadlax
interesting and delicious. Be bold with the dill!

Salad and Spinach Parcels

Dominic Tuffrey (son of Mike Tuffrey AM, Greater London Authority)

INGREDIENTS:
Baby spinach leaves (raw)
Pepper, any colour (small pieces)
Raisins or sultanas
Cashew nuts

FOR THE DRESSING:
1 tsp lemon juice
3tsp extra virgin olive oil
1 tsp runny honey
Salt and pepper

METHOD:
Put salad ingredients in a bowl.
Put dressing ingredients in a container with a lid and shake well.
Pour over salad. Toss well.

SPINACH PARCELS
Use the ingredients for the above salad.
Place on a large uncooked spinach leaf and fold over.

MIKE WRITES...
This dish was invented by Dominic, aged 7, who sometimes eats them.

Lettuce Soup

Chris Naylor, London Borough of Camden Councillor

INGREDIENTS:

2-3 chopped onions or shallots

1-2 medium garlic cloves, chopped

2-3 oz butter

1 tsp ground coriander or tarragon

½ tsp salt

¼ tsp fresh black pepper

1-2 medium potatoes, chopped small

½-1 lb coarsely chopped lettuce leaves

1 pint water

METHOD:

This soup is a great way to use lettuce's outer leaves and ribs.

Any kind of potato and lettuce or indeed spinach or watercress.

Cook chopped onions and garlic with butter on a low heat and stir until softened, 3 to 5 minutes.

Add coriander or tarragon, salt and pepper and stir for 1 minute.

Add potato, lettuce, water and bring to the boil.

Reduce heat and simmer, covered, until potato is very tender, about 15 minutes.

Puree soup in a sieve or blender.

Then bring soup to a simmer, season with salt and pepper to taste, or even add cream to taste.

CHRIS WRITES...

When I first came to Camden as a student, I stayed with a wonderful man, Miles Tomalin on Gloucester Avenue. He suggested I try for a job on the Fair Lady restaurant barge (which in fact went up and down the canal at the end of his garden). Without any advert or indeed interview that I can remember, I soon found myself crewing on the Fair Lady. The job fulfilled several of my needs. It was largely outdoors, it was paid, and indeed I got a meal on the back of the boat each time we went out. I can't remember much of the food but we almost always had lettuce soup, especially if there had not been much interest in salad the day before. I can't say it is my all-time favourite but it went on to feature on my own menu.

Mint or Coriander Dip

Lord Navnit Dholakia

INGREDIENTS:

1 bunch of fresh coriander
(mint can be a substitute)
1 large pot of plain yoghurt
4 tbls of desiccated coconut
2 tbls of sugar

2 medium size onions
1 tps of lemon juice
3-4 drops of green food colour
1 tsp of chilli powder

METHOD:

Remove roots from coriander or mint, keep both the stems and the leaves.
Put all the ingredients in a food processor until a smooth paste is obtained.

Good to dip with onion bhajis or samosas.

NAVNIT WRITES...

To this day I have not told this secret to my friends. A little while ago I
was invited by the Maharaja of Bhavnagar (my home state in India) for
Christmas dinner. He promised me that his chefs will produce the best
turkey I have ever eaten. True to his words, the Christmas dinner was
sumptuous. All the trimmings and you couldn't ask for more. It was only
after the feast that I realised that there were no turkeys in my part of the
world. Under gentle coaxing the truth was revealed. They had roasted a
majestic peacock. The national bird of India.

Mulligatawny Soup

Lord Dick Newby

INGREDIENTS:

½ lb onions chopped
½ level tbls mild curry powder
2 peeled chopped cloves of garlic
1 red pepper, sliced
8 oz red lentils

15oz can tomatoes
1 level tbls tomato puree
4 pints chicken stock
2 oz raisins
1 level tbls mild chilli powder

METHOD:
Cook onions gently in oil.
Add curry powder, garlic and pepper, cook for further 3 minutes.
Rinse lentils and drain well.
Rub tomatoes through a sieve to remove pips.
Add lentils and tomatoes and all other ingredients.
Season with salt and pepper.
Cook slowly for an hour.

DICK WRITES...
The ingredients are readily available and preparing this soup is essentially a matter of sorting out the ingredients and combining them. It doesn't take any great skill and always works. A great winter dish.

Roasted Peppers & Goats Cheese

Serves 4

Sarah Teather MP, Brent East

INGREDIENTS:

At least half a red pepper per person
1 packet of French crumbly goats cheese lots of basil, 1 pkt for 4
 people
Basil flavoured olive oil
Salt and pepper

METHOD:

Cut the peppers lengthwise into quarters and place them skin side up on a
oven baking tray.
Grill peppers until the skins turn black.
Leave to cool for a bit (about 10 minutes) before peeling off the skins.
Alternately, grill and peel the night before.
Wrap the peppers in foil with a little basil flavoured olive oil and leave in
fridge.
Chop the basil quite finely and stuff the peppers.
Then slice the cheese and put 1 slice on top of the basil.
Add a little salt and pepper and drizzle a little more basil oil on top.
Grill until the cheese turns brown (takes about 10 minutes)
Serve with warm crusty bread so people can mop up the juices afterwards.

SARAH WRITES...

The great thing about this recipe is you can do all the preparation ages
before people come round for dinner and then just finish it off while you
are chatting to your guests. I've never met anyone who does not like it and
it always looks very impressive but is in fact easy, which is ideal.

Spanish Gazpacho

Nick Clegg MP, Sheffield Hallam

INGREDIENTS:

10 plum tomatoes
1 cucumber
½ a green pepper
1 garlic clove

2 tbls wine vinegar
¾ cup of olive oil
½ cup of water
2 tsp salt

METHOD:

Peel and cut the tomatoes into quarters and the cucumber into chunks.
Blend the tomatoes, cucumber and pepper.
Add garlic, vinegar and water. Blend until it becomes thick.
Add olive oil, salt and re-blend.
Taste, add more vinegar or oil if you wish.
Pour the mixture through a strainer.
Refrigerate until cool, at least 30 minutes and ideally overnight.

Serve with croutons, little cubes of red pepper and cucumber and if you like onion.

NICK WRITES...

All quantities are approximate as there is no definitive recipe for Gazpacho. But this is my wife's so surely the best.

MAIN DISH

Beef Rendang

Serves 4

Baroness Shirley Williams of Crosby

INGREDIENTS:

For the pot

3 cans of coconut milk (low fat version is fine)

2 lbs of cubed beef (the long simmering makes the meat tender)

A lemon-grass stem, bruised and cut into small pieces

A few bay leaves (or Kaffir lime leaves if available)

1 tsp salt

For the paste

A thumb sized piece of fresh ginger, peeled and chopped

2 tsp turmeric

1 tsp paprika

3 chopped garlic cloves

2 chopped onions, preferably sweet (red onions work well)

Chilli powder (anything from ½ tsp to 2 tsp)

Some dried galingale (a Thai root spice, like ginger). Remove the dry
    pieces after cooking. If not available the dish works well without it.
    Finely grated peel of 1 lime.

METHOD:

Put all the paste ingredients in a blender and whiz into a fine paste adding a
little lemon or orange juice if required.

Put the pot ingredients in a large saucepan, ensuring the meat is completely
covered by the milk, add the paste.

Simmer for about 2 hours, uncovered, stirring occasionally. After this time
most of the liquid will have evaporated.

Continue cooking on low to medium heat, stirring frequently, until the dish
has become dry and thick and has absorbed all the remaining oil/liquid.

Serve with rice and vegetables, or as an alternative, mix with small cubes of
roasted sweet potato, green beans and a bunch of shredded fresh coriander.

SHIRLEY WRITES...

This is my favourite dish in Malaysia and I first tasted it when I visited my
daughter Rebecca in Kuala Lumpur in 1994. She and her husband lived
there for two years. The beef is simmered in coconut milk and spices,
absorbing the flavours and finishing as a crumbly, dark richly flavoured dry
dish. It works equally well in mild or spicy versions, and can also be done
with chicken.

Black Truffle Risotto with Sautéed Scallops and Wilted Spinach

Arthur Graves, London Borough of Camden Councillor

INGREDIENTS:
2 scallops with pink roe per person
About a couple of handfuls of spinach
250 gm Arborio rice
Salt and pepper
An egg yolk
Chicken stock, preferably home made
Good quality white wine
½ an onion, 2 cloves of garlic, ½ a stick of celery
2 heaped tsp of black truffle paste. I'd love to have written "Fresh
    Black Truffle" but we aren't Champagne Socialists now are we ?
Organic olive oil, not virgin or extra virgin

METHOD:
Finely chop the onion, garlic and celery. Sauté onion in olive oil for
2 minutes. Add garlic and celery and cook without colouring for
approximately 5 minutes.
Throw in the rice and stir round, cook on low heat for further couple of
minutes. Pour in white wine and stock in equal amounts, to just cover rice.
Turn up heat until it boils then turn right down and cook for about 5 mins.
Keep checking it until the rice has absorbed the liquid and when stirred
it looks kind of like rice pudding, but hopefully not as thick. It should have
some bite to it. Turn off the rice.
In a separate pan heat some oil till hot. Pop in the seasoned scallops, after
about a minute (if that) flip the little lovelies over.
Cook for another 30 seconds or so and remove from the pan.
Replace them with the washed spinach (please wash in a big bowl not a
colander). Cook for about 1 minute or so, moving the top leaves to the
bottom after 30 seconds. While the spinach is cooking, test the risotto for
seasoning, stir in 2 teaspoons of truffle paste and the egg yolk thoroughly.
Place wilted leaves in the middle of each plate, put 1 or 2 spoons of risotto
on top of the leaves (but not so as you completely cover them) and place
2 scallops on top of the risotto. If you garnish the dish with any sprigs of
parsley or some such, and add a dash of Balsamic vinegar or some other
sauce around the edges, I shall personally track you down and remove ALL
cooking implements from your home. Eat and Enjoy.

Casserole of Pheasant

Serves 4

Pamela, Countess of Listowel

INGREDIENTS:

I pheasant

I oz butter

I vacuum packed box or tin of chestnuts

½ lb button onions

¾ oz of flour (approximately)

¾-I pint of chicken stock

Grated rind and juice of 1/2 an orange

I dessertspoon red current jelly

I glass of red wine

METHOD:

Brown the pheasant in the butter, remove from pan.

Brown chestnuts and onions lightly, remove from pan.

Add enough flour to take up the fat.

Add the rest of the ingredients and bring to a gentle boil.

Add pheasant, chestnuts and onions.

Seasoning to taste.

Cook for I ½ hours.

Joint the bird and place on a dish along with the chestnuts and onions.
Skim the liquor and reduce if necessary.

A good accompaniment is a dish of Brussel sprouts sweated in butter with
a few chopped chestnuts and cream.

PAMELA WRITES...

I hope you have the good fortune to be given a pheasant which has been
shot and hung on the feather then plucked carefully.

Chicken Livers in Paprika Sauce

Serves 2

John Bryant, London Borough of Camden Councillor

INGREDIENTS:

Chicken livers for two about 400gm
A good glug of olive oil
1 medium onion
2 heaped tsp of paprika
Large pinches of dried basil

1 large tomato
Cornflour for dusting the livers
2 tsp chicken stock plus a cup of water
A good dash of Worcestershire sauce

METHOD:

Chop onion in small chunks.

Fry onion in olive oil over medium heat.

Add paprika and basil, stir and leave to soften onions.

Dust chicken livers in cornflour (if you want to remain gluten-free) cutting the larger ones into two through the gristly bits.

Add livers to frying pan adjusting the oil as the flour soaks this up.

Turn the livers over with prongs, lower heat during this operation.

Boil some water to skin the tomato.

Chop the tomato up and add to frying pan.

Mix some chicken stock with hot water and add to frying pan, with a good dash of Worcestershire sauce.

Add lid if you have one and simmer for 10 minutes only, regularly turning the livers to make sure they are cooked.

You should end up with a remarkably thick spicy gravy which is a superb winter warmer.

Can be served with mashed potato or, if you are on a carbohydrate free diet try serving with mixed salad leaves sprinkled with balsamic vinegar.

JOHN WRITES...

If your memory of liver is bits of leather served at school loosely described as pigs liver, think again. This stuff melts in your mouth and is the ultimate meat-eaters comfort food. This is a quick recipe to give you a hot dinner or lunch in about 15 minutes. It's for councillors like me who like to have good meals but have no time to cook.

Cider Pork Chops and Stuffing

Serves 4

David Laws MP, Yeovil

INGREDIENTS:

2 pork chops, trimmed of
any rind or fat
Real cider (dry or medium)
3-4 potatoes depending on size
½ a swede
2-3 carrots,
1 medium onion

2-3 leeks
2 large flat 'field' mushrooms
Freshly ground black pepper
Cornflour for thickening the
sauce
1 packet sage and onion stuffing

METHOD:

Preheat the oven to 180°C, 350°F, gas mark 4.

Make up the stuffing as instructed and set aside.

Wash the chops well to remove any bone fragments and pat dry with kitchen towel.

Peel and dice the swede and carrots. Peel and slice the onion.

Wash, trim and slice the leeks and flat mushrooms.

Wash and peel the potatoes and cut into ¼" or 6mm thick slices.

Put the diced and sliced swede, carrots, onions, leeks and mushrooms into a casserole. Add pepper.

Layer the sliced potatoes over the mixed vegetables.

Spread the stuffing evenly over the chops.

Pour the cider over the vegetables until it reaches the top layer of the potatoes. Lay the stuffing covered chops on top of the potatoes.

Cover the dish with the lid and place into the centre of the oven.

Cook for about 1 hour and then remove the lid for the last 15-20 minutes or so. If you require the stuffing to be crispy place casserole under a grill for about 6 minutes. Remove the chops and the vegetables from the dish and keep warm. Strain liquor from the vegetables into a saucepan (not all the liquid should be used).

Add ¼-½ pint medium or sweet cider to the liquor, thicken to taste with cornflour. Bring to the boil, simmer for a couple of minutes and add seasoning if you wish.

Always ensure that the pork meat is thoroughly cooked. Cooking times vary depending on the size of the pork chops and the oven specifications.

Cod in Orange and Passion Fruit Sauce

Serves 2

Laurie Millward, Camden Liberal Democrat

INGREDIENTS:

2 fresh cod fillets with
or without the skin left
on or 4 smaller pre-packed
chilled cod fillets
1 orange
2 passion fruit

1 small onion or 2 shallots
4 tbls Greek yoghurt or
fromage blanc
Salt and pepper
Optional — a garnish of herbs
and capers

METHOD:

Grate zest from orange and squeeze the juice.
Cut passion fruit in half and rub the contents through a sieve.
Mix together the juice from the orange and the passion fruit.
Reserve a dessertspoon of the passion fruit pulp and the seeds for garnish.
Add the rest to the marinade. Peel and thinly slice the onion or shallots.
Season cod fillets and place them, skin side up, in the marinade for 30-40 mins.
Place fish under a very hot grill, skin side up, for 8-10 minutes, depending
on the thickness of the fish.
Strain the marinade into a shallow pan and reduce it until syrupy.
Beat in the yoghurt or fromage fraîche to thicken it.
When the sauce is heated through divide it into two and lay a piece of fish
alongside.
Garnish with herbs, capers and the passion fruit pulp and seeds.
Serve with small new potatoes tossed in a little butter and green salad with
a simple French dressing.

ABOUT LAURIE...

Laurie, who died in November 2006, was a long standing member of West
Hampstead and Fortune Green Liberal Democrats in the London Borough
of Camden. She was a key element in all local fund-raising events and
election day organisation. Before moving to London in the seventies she
had been a Liberal councillor in Hull and a Parliamentary candidate in the
1966 Hull by-election. She loved to entertain and took enormous care with
every element of a dinner party.

Lamb Koftas (meatballs)

Serves 4

Sajjad Karim MEP, North West of England

INGREDIENTS:

450gm (1 lb) lean minced ground lamb
2 tsp ginger paste
2 tsp garlic pulped
4 fresh green chillis, finely chopped
1 small onion finely chopped
1 egg
½ tsp turmeric
1 tsp garam masala
50gm/2oz/2 cups fresh coriander (chopped)
4-6 fresh mint leaves chopped or ½ tsp mint sauce
175gm/6oz potato
Salt to taste
Vegetable oil for deep frying

METHOD:

Place the first ten ingredients in a bowl.
Grate the potato into the bowl and season with salt.
Knead together to blend well and form a soft dough.
Shape the mixture into portions the size of golf balls.
Set aside on a plate and leave the koftas to rest about 25 minutes.
Heat the oil to medium hot and fry the koftas in small batches until they are golden brown in colour.
Drain well and serve hot.

Lancashire Hot Pot

Serves 4

Lord Tom McNally of Blackpool

INGREDIENTS:

1½ lbs middle or best   ¼ pint of water
  end of lamb   Meat dripping
Salt and pepper
2 large potatoes
2 carrots
1 large onion or 2 leeks
1 small turnip

METHOD:

Pre-heat the oven to 150°C, 300°F, gas mark 2

Season the lamb with salt and pepper.

Peel and thickly slice the potatoes, turnip, carrots, and onion.

If using leeks cut into 1 inch pieces.

Place the lamb, potatoes, carrots, turnip and onion in layers in a deep casserole.

Add more salt and pepper to taste.

End with an overlapping layer of potato.

Add enough of the water to reach about a third of the way up the casserole.

Place small pats of meat dripping on top of the potatoes.

Cover the casserole and cook for 2½ - 3 hours.

Remove cover about 30 minutes before the end of cooking time and increase heat to (200°C, 400°F, gas mark 6) to brown the top layers of potatoes.

Serve with pickled red cabbage.

TOM WRITES...

You will not be surprised if my contribution is "Lancashire Hot Pot". Like all exiles, food can rekindle memories of home and childhood long ago. To me Hot Pot is as Lancashire as Gracie Fields or, dare I say it, Sir Cyril Smith!

Mediterranean Pot Roast Chicken

Lord Tim Garden

INGREDIENTS:
- 1 free-range chicken
- 2 whole garlic heads
- Bay leaves, thyme, rosemary
- 175ml dry sherry
- Sherry vinegar
- Olive oil
- Seasoning

METHOD:

Clean any excess fat off the chicken and season it inside and out.
Heat 2 tbls of olive oil in a casserole just large enough to take the chicken.
Fry the chicken in the hot oil until the skin is light brown on all sides.
Turn the heat down to low, and rest the chicken on one side in the pot.
Add the 2 garlic heads broken into cloves but not peeled.
Put in the herbs, add the sherry and a tbls of sherry vinegar.
Cover and cook for 25 minutes
Turn the chicken over to rest on the other side in the liquid, and replace the cover.
Cook for another 20 minutes.

Serve the chicken on a carving dish, and sieve the liquid to provide the sauce. Fried potatoes in butter and peas go well with this dish.

ABOUT TIM...

Apart from being an authoritative voice in the House of Lords and a serviceman with a very distinguished record, Tim was very active in Camden Liberal Democrats and served in his capacity as President of the local party with characteristic good humour and vigour. We miss him greatly.
When he suggested this recipe he added: "This is a dish that takes a few minutes to prepare, and less than an hour to cook. The smell of garlic and herbs makes the mouth water while waiting for it to be ready."

Moroccan Chicken, or Lamb

Helen and Roger Martyn, Camden Liberal Democrats

INGREDIENTS:

2 tbls olive oil

4 cloves of garlic (crushed)

1½ lbs boneless, skinless chicken breast, or a tender cut of lamb, cut into large bite size pieces

1½ tsp grill seasoning blend and/or salt and coarse pepper

2 medium yellow skinned onions, quartered and sliced

10 pitted prunes, coarsely chopped

1oz golden raisins

2 cups chicken stock, low sodium or organic if possible

Spice blend as you wish, but, for example, 1½ tsp of both cumin and sweet paprika, ½ tsp of both coriander and turmeric and a little cinnamon

METHOD:

Heat a large non-stick pan over a medium high heat.

Add the olive oil and the garlic.

Season meat with the seasoning blend and scatter around the pan.

Cook for 2 minutes on each side to brown, then add onions, prunes, raisins, and stock.

Mix the spices and scatter over the pot.

Cover and reduce to medium heat.

Cook for about 8 minutes stirring once or twice.

Remove the lid of the pot and cook for another few minutes to thicken slightly, adjust seasoning to taste.

Serve with couscous and garnish with chopped cilantro or flat leaf parsley and your choice of chutney. Mango goes well. This dish can also be partly cooked in the oven and if you have a tagine it adds to the Moroccan ambience.

Pork Fillet Stuffed with Garlic and Apple Sauce Wrapped in Parma Ham

Serves 4

Dee Doocey AM, Greater London Authority

INGREDIENTS:

2 pork fillets (each about 8-10 inches long)
4 large cloves of garlic
One jar of apple sauce

12 slices of Parma ham
One bottle of dry Riesling
Freshly ground salt and pepper

METHOD:

Prehead oven to 180°C, 350°F, gas mark 4.

Crush the garlic cloves and mix thoroughly with about 6 tbls of apple sauce. Lay out six slices of Parma ham overlapping each other, so that the width matches the length of one pork fillet.

Using a sharp knife cut down the length of one pork fillet, almost all the way through, so that you have created a pocket.

Spoon in some of the garlic and apple mixture — not too much as it will spill out. Close up the pork fillet and lay on top of the Parma ham.

Wrap the fillet in the ham — it will stick to itself so you do not have to tie it up. Repeat with second fillet. Heat some oil in a large oval casserole dish, and cook the pork fillets on all sides until the Parma ham is golden (this won't take more than about 30 seconds on each side).

Once the fillets have a nice colour all over, add a small amount of wine and, without removing the pork, briskly stir the bottom of the pan to pick up any residue. Then add the remainder of the apple sauce and garlic mixture and enough of the wine so that the liquid reaches halfway up the pork fillets. (You may now drink the rest of the wine)

Put the lid on the casserole, and place in pre-heated oven for 25-30 mins.

Checking that the pork is cooked through, remove the fillets from the casserole dish and place on a carving board to rest.

Put the casserole back on the hob, and reduce the sauce by about a third. You can also add any juices that flow from the pork.

Carve the pork fillets into slices and arrange on a serving platter, pour the sauce over, and serve with new potatoes and whichever green vegetable is in season.

Roti de Noix Gratiné à la Provençale (or Nut Bake)

Serves 6

Alexis Rowell, London Borough of Camden Councillor

INGREDIENTS:

Several good slugs of olive oil
2-3 cloves of garlic roughly chopped or chilli if you like it hot
I shallot or ordinary onion or 1/2 a leek roughly chopped
2 handfuls of mixed nuts. If you use Brazil nuts break into pieces
½ a tin of tomatoes and ½ a tin of mixed beans, you can also use
   dried beans but make sure you soak and cook them first
A glass or two of white wine or two large shots of vodka or the
   juice of a lemon or both, or neither
2-3 stalks of celery (separate the leaves if any and put them to one
   side) or a courgette or both, chopped
A large handful of spinach or other green leaf vegetable like kale
4-5 medium sized potatoes, washed and sliced but not peeled
400gm of grated or sliced cheddar, gruyere, Emmental or goats cheese
3 handfuls of mixed fresh herbs, preferably from your own garden

METHOD:

Combine the olive oil, garlic, nuts and onion or leek in a medium size
casserole dish. Cook for a few minutes over a medium flame then add the
alcohol. Let it bubble for a few minutes, then add the tomatoes and celery.
Leave it to simmer while you wash the potatoes and cut into thin slices.
Mix the sliced courgette and beans and lemon juice in with the rest, turn
off the heat. Now add a layer of uncooked spinach or kale and the celery
leaves. Then add several layers of sliced potatoes. Pop the lid on and put in
oven for 30 minutes. Add the grated or sliced cheese, then put back in oven
for 15 minutes or until the cheese is starting to brown.
Serve on a bed of mixed herbs. I've used rocket, oregano, lemon balm, basil
and nasturtium. The final touch in our household is always a topping of
mixed organic herbs.

ALEXIS WRITES...

It's a little known fact that the main reason I joined the Lib Dems was
because of the party's excellent Food Policy. I love food and I love cooking.
But I'm also passionate about the politics of food. I try to buy organic
wherever possible and do not buy food that has been flown into the country.

Smoked Haddock Pie

Serves 6

Rt Hon Sir Menzies Campbell CBE QC MP, Fife North East

INGREDIENTS:

½ lb spinach (fresh or frozen)
1 lb smoked haddock, cooked and flaked
6 tomatoes peeled and sliced
6 hard boiled eggs sliced
Cheese sauce

METHOD:

Butter an oven-proof dish and layer the ingredients in it.
Starting with the spinach, then the haddock, the hard boiled eggs and finally the tomatoes.
Season with salt and pepper between each layer.
Finally cover with the cheese sauce.
Heat in a moderate oven for 30 minutes.

MING WRITES...

Elspeth and I love entertaining and good food. A good dinner party involves much chat and conviviality. The advantage of this dish is that it can be prepared in advance and kept warm for when the conversation overtakes the timings of the meal.

Toad in the Hole

Edward Davey MP, Kingston and Surbiton

INGREDIENTS:

Good quality sausages (pork probably suits this dish best, but to taste)

110 gm (4oz) plain white flour

300 ml (½ pint) milk

2 small eggs

½ tsp salt

METHOD:

Preheat the oven to 230°C, 450°F, gas mark 8

Place the flour in a bowl, then make a well in the centre and break in the egg. Mix in half the milk using a wooden spoon, work the mixture until smooth. Then add the remaining milk.

Beat or whisk until fully combined and the surface is covered with tiny bubbles. Allow to rest for 15-30 minutes, whisk again before use.

Fry the sausages in a pan to lightly colour and remove excess fat, reserve the fat. Place the fat in a small roasting tin adding a little oil, if needed, to bring the amount of fat up to 4 tbls.

Heat the fat until smoking hot then pour in the batter.

Cut the sausages in half and place into the hot oven.

Bake for about 5-10 minutes, then reduce to 200°C, 400°F, Gas mark 6 and bake for a further 20-30 minutes or until the batter has risen and is a deep golden brown.

Serve immediately or the pudding will deflate.

ED WRITES...

I adore Yorkshire Pudding and Toad in the Hole. The best way of indulging this is as the equivalent of a Sunday roast! When she was widowed, my mum had to feed three growing boys on not a lot, so she excelled at this type of meal. I doubt it gets in any low fat recipe book, but with top grade sausages and some onion gravy, you can't go wrong.

DESSERTS

The Best Cheesecake in the World

Baroness Julia Neuberger

INGREDIENTS:

2 tubs cream cheese
3 tubs curd cheese or thick
quark
75-100gm sugar (to taste)
4 large eggs
1 tsp vanilla essence

Topping
2 tubs creamed smetana
1 tsp sugar
1 tsp vanilla essence

METHOD:

Preheat the oven to 150°C, 300°F, gas mark 2.
Cream together the cream cheese, curd cheese, eggs, sugar and vanilla essence.
When creamy and smooth, taste and add more sugar if required.
Pour into a loose bottom 9 inch cake tin.
Place tin on a baking tray as it is inclined to drip.
Bake for approximately 50 minutes.
Meanwhile, mix smetana, 2 tsp sugar and 1 tsp vanilla essence.
Carefully put on top of the cake and bake at 225°C, 430°F, gas mark 7-8 for 10 minutes.
Take out and leave to cool.
Best after 12 hours.
Refrigerate after 24 hours.

JULIA WRITES...

The best cheesecake in the world. I prefer to use an old fashioned Kenwood Mixer with a K beater to make it.

Chocolate Mousse

Serves 4 (or 1 chocoholic)

Mark Pack, Head of Innovations, Liberal Democrats

INGREDIENTS:

175 gm chocolate
3 medium eggs
1 chocolate flake

METHOD:

Break up the chocolate and place it in an oven proof bowl.
Add a tbls of water.
Place bowl in oven (set to low) and leave about 10 minutes for the chocolate to melt.
Separate the eggs.
Mix the yolks together and then add the melted chocolate.
Beat with a fork until they are thoroughly mixed.
Whip the egg whites until they are firm.
Dollop the egg whites on top of the mixture.
Carefully mix, using a slow cutting and folding motion.
When the mixture is of a uniform colour, serve into 4 bowls.
Put in fridge to set, at least an hour.

Crumble the chocolate flake into pieces on top of each bowl and serve.

Christmas Pudding

Mike Pringle MSP, Edinburgh South and Lothians

INGREDIENTS:

110 gm plain flour
110 gm breadcrumbs
80 gm suet
110 gm brown sugar
110 gm sultanas
60 gm currants
60 gm raisins
1 cooking apple, grated

275ml milk
1 egg
2 tbls treacle
Pinch of salt, nutmeg and
    cinnamon
50 ml brandy
1 tsp baking powder

METHOD:

Mix the ingredients together in a large bowl.
Transfer to a heat proof glass bowl.
Cover with a circle of greaseproof paper and tie with string.
Put in a steamer and cook for 2hrs.

Serve in warmed pudding bowls with warm brandy cream

MIKE WRITES...

I think this is the best Christmas pudding recipe not too sweet but delicious

Danish Crisp

Serves 6

Lady Sue Garden

INGREDIENTS:

Biscuit
4 oz (125gm) caster sugar
4 oz (125gm) ground
almonds
4 oz (125gm) butter
2 dessertspoons (20gm) plain
flour
4 tbls (60ml) single cream

Filling
1 oz (25gm) grated or chopped bitter
chocolate
3 slices fresh or tinned pineapple,
chopped finely
½ pint double cream
1 dessertspoon (10gm) caster sugar
1 tbls (15ml) brandy (optional)

METHOD:
Preheat the oven to 180°C, 350°F, gas mark 4

Biscuit
Put all ingredients in a saucepan.
Mix gently over a low heat until butter and sugar have melted.
Spread mixture thinly in 2 equal size circles on 2 lightly greased baking
sheets (they will spread while they cook).
Bake for 15-20 minutes in medium oven.
Watch very carefully and remove when they are toffee brown.
Neaten up the edges while still hot or warm. Once cool they should be
crisp and brittle.
Loosen from the baking sheet while still warm, leave until cold.

Filling
Whip cream, fold in sugar, pineapple, chocolate and brandy if required.
Pile onto one of the biscuits and cover with the second biscuit.
Decorate with sieved icing sugar.

SUE WRITES...
This is a simple and delicious dessert. The biscuit makes a brandy snap
sandwich with a creamy middle. The biscuit can be made in advance if kept
in an airtight tin, otherwise it goes soft which still tastes good. You can use
different fruits for the filling but pineapple has a sharpness which offsets the
richness of the other ingredients.

Dream Cream

Vivienne Joffe, Camden Liberal Democrats

INGREDIENTS:
1 cup thick sour cream, crème fraîche or smetana
1 cup seedless green grapes
¾ cup chopped marshmallows (I use the mini ones to avoid
    chopping)
½ cup well drained chopped pineapple
½ cup desiccated coconut
½ cup tinned or fresh guavas, peaches, apricots, etc

METHOD:
Combine all ingredients and pile into a pretty dish.
Refrigerate overnight.
Alternately place in a mould, freeze for 8 hrs, turn out and garnish as
desired.

Marianne's Port Jelly

Flick Rea, London Borough of Camden Councillor

INGREDIENTS:
1 bottle of RUBY port
(not always easy to get but don't make it with tawny port)
2½ sachets of powdered gelatine
(3 makes it too stiff and 2 makes it too long to set)
120 gm (4oz) caster sugar
Pinch grated nutmeg
Pinch grated cinnamon
2 tsp of lemon juice

METHOD:
Soak the gelatine in a quarter of the port and all the lemon juice until softened.
Then add another quarter of port, the spices and the sugar.
Heat gently bringing almost to the boil stirring constantly until gelatine has completely dissolved.
Strain through a fine sieve (preferably lined with muslin)
Cool slightly and then stir in the remaining port.
Pour into mould to set.

Before serving you can decorate with whipped cream, nuts or my favourite, tiny ratafia

FLICK WRITES...
This popular (originally Victorian) recipe was introduced to me about ten years ago and fast became a favourite. I make it at Christmas instead of Christmas pudding and always at parties. The recipe has proved a great favourite with friends from the States and the recipe has crossed the Atlantic several times! It is very rich and not everyone's taste, but aficionados keep coming back for it !

I think you are supposed to make it in a fluted jelly mould, but I just make it in a bowl, it tastes just as good!

Mincemeat Ice-Cream

Margaret Smith MSP, Edinburgh West
Suzanne Smith-Main

INGREDIENTS:
>   3oz mincemeat (3 or 4 tbls)
>   4 egg yolks
>   4oz caster sugar
>   ½ pint of milk
>   ½ pint double cream

METHOD:
Slowly heat the milk in a saucepan to boiling point.
Beat the egg yolks and sugar together, and whilst still beating pour on the milk.
Put mixture back into pan on a low heat.
Stir consistently until there is a film over the back of the spoon.
Do not boil or it will all separate horribly!
Cool thoroughly, mix in the cream and the mincemeat and then freeze.

MARGARET WRITES...
It's quite yummy !

Russian Cream

Julia Goldsworthy MP, Falmouth and Camborne

INGREDIENTS:
1 pint milk
4 oz sugar
2 eggs
1 oz (1 sachet) gelatine
A few drops of almond or vanilla essence

METHOD:
Mix sugar, gelatine powder, egg yolks and a little cold water.
Warm milk to blood heat, add to sugar mixture.
Return to heat, bring to boil and simmer for 5 minutes.
Leave to cool right down.
Whisk egg whites until stiff and fold into the milk mixture.
Add a few drops of almond or vanilla essence.
Leave in a cool place to set for approximately 2 hours.

JULIA WRITES...
A lovely traditional Cornish recipe!

Sherry Trifle

Keith Moffitt, Leader London Borough of Camden

INGREDIENTS:

1 packet trifle sponges or plain sponge cake
1 small packet amaretti biscuits or ratafias
Tin of apricots or peaches (use as many as desired)
Quince or bramble jelly (or jam) to spread over sponges
Custard using 1 heaped tbls of custard powder to ½ pint of milk
  (more if larger bowl)
Sherry glass of home made liqueur (or sherry)
Pot of whipping cream

METHOD:

Halve the trifle sponges and half again.
Spread jelly or jam on top and place at bottom of trifle bowl.
Add amaretti biscuits or ratafias, slightly crushed, on top.
Add a layer of sliced fruit.
Repeat the layers, the amount of layers depending on the size of the trifle
bowl or until all the trifle sponges are used.
Pour over about half the juice from the tin of fruit.
Add the glass of liqueur.
Make custard and pour over trifle and leave to cool.
Cover with a tea cloth to prevent a skin forming.
When the trifle is cold, whip the cream until stiff and spoon onto the trifle.
Decorate with chocolate strands.

KEITH WRITES...

I love trifle and would like to thank Pam Latchford for her recipe from
'Ludlow Puddings'

Summer Fruit Brulée

Serve 6

Jim Wallace QC, former MSP for Orkney and Shetland and Deputy First Minister of Scotland 1999-2005

INGREDIENTS:

I tub 450 gm frozen raspberries
I tub 450 gm frozen summer fruits (or a second tub of raspberries)
I large tub of Greek Yoghurt
250ml whipping cream
2 tbls cornflour
Granulated sugar
Icing sugar

METHOD:

Put raspberries and 4 tbls granulated sugar in a pan and bring slowly to the boil stirring continuously. Remove from heat.

Mix the cornflour with a small amount of water and add to the raspberry mixture. Return to the heat and simmer for 30 seconds.

Add the tub of summer fruits to the raspberry mixture and put into a shallow bowl. Put in fridge for at least an hour to set.

Put the cream in a bowl with a level tbls of icing sugar and whip until the cream thickens. Fold the Greek yoghurt into the cream, spread on top of the fruit mixture.

Put 6 tbls of granulated sugar and a small amount of water in a heavy bottomed pan. Bring to the boil and boil until the mixture starts to darken. Control the heat until the mixture is dark brown being careful not to let it burn. Remove from heat and drizzle over the top of the cream and yoghurt. Leave in the fridge until ready to serve.

If possible make the brulée topping within an hour of serving as it tends to soften.

JIM WRITES...

This delicious pudding can bring a taste of summer to the wildest and darkest winter day and year- round it brings the health benefits of red berries. And if the fruit comes from the famous Scottish berry fields, it will taste even better.

Surprise Cream Pots

Serves 4

Deirdre Razzall, editor Liberal Democrat News

INGREDIENTS:
>Any of the following fruit: white grapes halved and deseeded,
>clementine segments, halved strawberries, blueberries or even
>stewed apples with sultanas
>Double cream
>Demerara sugar

METHOD:
Half fill some little pots or ramekins with fruit of choice.
Whip double cream until it stands in peaks.
Spoon over the fruit until it reaches almost the top.
Chill, covered with cling film until ready to serve.
Before serving heat the grill, remove the cling film.
Carefully put a thick layer of demerara sugar to completely cover the top
of the cream.
Place pots under a hot grill for 1-2 minutes (watching all the time).
Take out when the sugar has melted and is bubbling.

If preferred this dish can be made in a gratin dish, but your guests will not
have the surprise of finding the fruit hiding under the cream.

DEIRDRE WRITES...
Puddings are not my thing. An unfortunate incident with a meringue when
I was 15 years old, could possibly have been the cause. I was having tea in
a café with my godmother. After chasing this large white blob around the
plate with one of those two-pronged dessert forks, I made the mistake of
picking it up. One bite and my whole face was covered by an explosion of
cream and white, fluffy meringue bits. The café and my godmother were
highly amused; I didn't eat the horrid things again for nearly 30 years.

Tiramisu

Flick Rea, London Borough of Camden Councillor

INGREDIENTS:

100 ml (3½ fluid ounces) strong black coffee
60 gm (2 oz) caster sugar
6 tbls Marsala or sweet sherry (or brandy will do)
1 packet of sponge finger biscuits
3 eggs (separated)
Good pinch of nutmeg
250 gm (8 oz) mascarpone
Chocolate grated to decorate

METHOD:

Stir half the sugar into the coffee and add the Marsala.
Arrange half the biscuits in the bottom of a serving dish and drizzle over half the coffee mixture.
Beat the egg yolks with the remaining sugar, until stiff.
Fold in the mascarpone mixture and spoon half of it over the biscuits.
Dip the remaining biscuits into the remaining coffee mixture, arrange on top.
Cover with the remaining mascarpone mixture and smooth.
Keep in fridge until needed.
Before serving sprinkle with grated chocolate.

FLICK WRITES...

I have always said that I founded a political career on food — particularly puddings!

Wanstead Brandy Cake

Laura Noel, Camden Liberal Democrat

INGREDIENTS:

8 oz digestive biscuits	3 oz caster sugar
8 oz plain chocolate	2 oz glace cherries
8 oz butter	2 oz walnuts
2 eggs	2 tbls brandy

METHOD:

Crush the digestive biscuits coarsely.
Melt the chocolate with the sugar.
Beat the eggs and sugar together until creamy.
Then beat in the chocolate and the butter.
Fold in the cherries, walnuts, brandy and biscuits.
Put in a 7 inch loose bottom tin.
Decorate with more cherries and nuts.
Put in fridge for half an hour.

LAURA WRITES...

I was given this wonderful cake recipe by the male Matron of Wanstead Hospital in the East End when I was a young manager there. Several moves and many years later I became the Chief Executive Officer of the Health Authority for the area. More to the point this cake is wicked and easy.

Wicked Ice Cream

Ed Fordham, PPC Hampstead and Kilburn

INGREDIENTS:
570ml double cream
1 tin of condensed milk
Fudge (enough for about 14 chunks ½ inch wide)

METHOD:
Beat the cream until very stiff (almost over-whipped)
Then stir in the condensed milk until the mixture comes back to a creamy texture.
Cut the fudge into chunks.
Stir into the mixture and freeze.

If you don't like fudge any sort of chocolate will do just as well.

ED WRITES...
This is a huge favourite with all ages (and a cook's favourite because there's none of the fuss about taking it out of the fridge and re-beating it and refreezing). It's dead easy.

TEA TIME

Apple Cake

David Abrahams, London Borough of Camden Councillor

INGREDIENTS:

5oz (150gm) butter

2 large eggs

8oz (225gm) caster sugar

1 tsp (5ml) almond essence

8oz (225gm) self-raising flour

1½ level tsp baking powder

1½ lb (675gm) cooking apples, before peeling

Icing sugar to sprinkle on finished cake

METHOD:

Heat the oven to 375°F, 190°C, gas mark 5.

Grease well a 9 or 10 inch loose-bottom cake tin.

Melt the butter over a medium heat until just runny and pour into a big bowl.

Add the eggs, sugar and almond essence and beat well until mixed.

Fold in the flour and baking powder.

Spread just under two thirds of the mixture in the cake tin.

Peel, core and slice the apples and arrange roughly on top of the mixture.

Spread remaining mixture over apples.

The mixture may not cover all the apples.

Bake for 1-1½ hours. (in my fan oven 1 hour is plenty), until the apple is tender. Loosen the side of the cake with a knife and gently push the cake out. Dust over generously with icing sugar when slightly cooled.

Serve warm or cold with lots of lightly whipped or thick cream.

Keep covered in fridge and eat within 4 days but you will probably find it goes quicker that that.

DAVID WRITES...

Don't worry, the recipe does work! My mum was given a photocopy of this recipe years ago, not sure where it came from originally. Since then, it's become a great favourite, made for lots of family celebrations. It always disappears very quickly.

Astrid's Oatcakes

Donald Gorrie, MSP for Central Scotland Region 1997-2007

INGREDIENTS:

> 2 teacups of medium oatmeal
> 1/2 tsp bicarbonate of soda
> 1/4 tsp of salt
> A knob of melted dripping (or less than a tsp of olive oil)

METHOD:

Preheat the oven to 180°C, 350°F, gas mark 2

Mix all the ingredients in a bowl.

Add sufficient (nearly boiled) water to bind everything together.

Don't make the mixture sloppy.

Take small quantities at a time, cover with dry oatmeal and roll out very thin.

Place on a baking tin and cook for about 20 minutes, or until the edges just begin to turn pale brown.

To keep them flat turn over half way through the cooking time.

DONALD WRITES...

These oatcakes are delicious with butter and marmalade, cheese or honey and easy enough for anyone to make.

Australian Shortbread

Andrew Stunell MP, Hazel Grove

INGREDIENTS:

 250gm rolled oats (or 150gm oats and 100gm any kind of flour)
 125gm soft margarine
 75gm white sugar

METHOD:

Preheat the oven to 180°C, 350°F, gas mark 4.

Cream the fat and the sugar with a wooden spoon.

Add the oats or oats and flour and work into the mixture with the fingers.

Put the mixture into a greased square or oblong tin and flatten it down well.

Bake for around half an hour.

Stand until almost cold and cut into fingers.

This recipe is quite tolerant and can be cooked in a cooler oven for longer if you want to cook it along side other things. A hotter oven scorches it at the edges.

ANDREW WRITES...

Australian shortbread (but we call it Oatycake) is better than cake, and a feast and a festival special in our house. Our children have all made it at one time or another standing on a chair in the kitchen, with light supervision. So it is really very simple, and quite forgiving of measurement fluctuations. Enjoy!

Canvassing Biscuits

Serves 4

Paul Burstow MP, Sutton and Cheam

INGREDIENTS:
>   10oz self raising flour
>   4oz cooking margarine
>   4 oz sugar
>   2 tbls of golden syrup

METHOD:
Preheat the oven to 180°C, 350°F, gas mark 4.

Rub the self raising flour and margarine, until they look like bread crumbs.
Add the sugar.

Warm the golden syrup in a pan until it is gently runny, but not boiling hot.

Add the self raising flour, margarine and sugar to the golden syrup.

Stir well to form a doughy ball.

Roll out and, using a round cutter, cut out the biscuits.

Bake in a medium oven on a greased tray for about 8 minutes, till pale brown.

Feel free at the doughy ball stage to add lemon juice and zest, ground ginger, dried fruit or flaked almonds to create whatever flavour you fancy.

PAUL WRITES...

These are extremely tasty when offered to people after a hard night's canvassing together with a warming cup of tea or coffee

Flapjacks

Serves 4

Mick Bates AM, National Assembly for Wales

INGREDIENTS:

4 oz soft brown sugar
5 oz butter
2 rounded tbls golden syrup
6 oz whole oats
1 oz desiccated coconut
2 oz quartered cherries

METHOD:

Preheat the oven to 150°C, 300°F, gas mark 2.

Lightly grease a baking tin 8 inches at least and 1½ inches deep.

Place sugar, butter and syrup together in a saucepan and heat gently until the fat has melted, then stir.

Take the pan off the heat and stir in all the other ingredients, mixing thoroughly.

Pour the mixture into the prepared tin and press it down evenly.

Bake in the centre of the oven for 40-45 minutes.

Allow the mixture to cool in the tin for 10 minutes before cutting into bars.

Leave until quite cold before removing from the tin.

MICK WRITES...

Children can make these very easily and they are much healthier than shop-bought biscuits!

Lemon Flan

Serves 4

Janet Grauberg, London Borough of Camden Councillor

INGREDIENTS:

1 small pkt biscuits (digestive or ginger nut)
1 large tin (14oz) condensed milk
3 large lemons
Butter to melt
1 large (10oz) pot double cream

METHOD:

Crush biscuits (put in a biodegradable polythene bag and attack violently)
Melt lots of butter in a pan and mix in the crushed biscuits (still on the heat) until it starts to form small lumps.
Press the biscuits down into a flan or quiche base so they are spread evenly over the base.
Leave overnight or at least three hours.
Rind and then squeeze the lemons.
Put into a mixing bowl the ingredients in the following order.
Condensed milk, lemon rind, cream, lemon juice.
Stir briefly and spoon over the flan base so it is evenly spread.
Chill in the fridge for about three hours.
Decorate, for example with sliced kiwi fruit of strawberry halves.

JANET WRITES...

People who know me will not be surprised to know that I have three bulging files of recipes that I have collected from friends and relations. This is the first recipe that I was given while a student and is therefore the foundation of my personal recipe collection. I still consider it my "signature dish" and still make it whenever I'm asked to contribute a pudding to an event. It is simple, delicious and extremely fattening!

BD Littlejohn's Chocolate Cake

Nicol Stephen MSP, Aberdeen South

INGREDIENTS:

4 oz self raising flour
5 oz caster sugar
4 oz soft margarine
2 eggs
1 tbls milk
1 heaped tbls chocolate powder

Topping

3 oz cooking chocolate
3 oz soft margarine
1½ oz caster sugar
1½ dessertspoons of milk
3 dessertspoons of hot water

METHOD:

Pre-heat oven to 160°C, 325°F, gas mark 4

Mix together all cake ingredients for 2-3 minutes.

Turn into a very well greased cake tin (2 regular sandwich tins or a 7"x11" rectangle tin).

Bake for 30-40 minutes.

Topping

Melt chocolate and whisk margarine and sugar into chocolate.

Add water and milk then allow to cool a little and whisk until thick.

Spread topping over sponge and create a rippled effect with a fork.

Grated chocolate may be scattered on the top.

NICHOL WRITES...

This recipe was given to me by a family friend, BD Littlejohn. She was a lovely cheery and very busy Liberal Democrat lady who sadly died in 2003. She was an original member of the "Carrot Club" which my wife helped to organise. The club brought together members and supporters across Aberdeen South on a weekly basis for cake and campaigning!

Microwave Carrot Cake

Sidney Malin, Camden Liberal Democrat

INGREDIENTS:

¼ pint sunflower oil
8 oz brown sugar
3 large eggs
6 oz (or a little more) self-
raising flour
1 tsp bicarbonate of soda
2 tsp (or more to taste) cinnamon
Some nutmeg (optional)
3 large carrots grated
4 oz walnut halves chopped

Icing
1 third of a litre cream or curd
cheese
The rind of 1 lemon
1 tsp lemon juice
2 tsp icing sugar (or more to
taste)

METHOD:

Beat together the sunflower oil, brown sugar and 3 large eggs.

Add flour, bicarbonate of soda, cinnamon, nutmeg, carrots and walnuts and beat again.

Put into 8" casserole or soufflé dish (grease well, line bottom of dish with waxed paper).

Cook on medium Microwave for 24 minutes.

Mix ingredients for topping well.

When cool cut cake into 3 parts.
Ice each layer LIBERALLY.
Ice top and sides LIBERALLY.

Decorate with walnuts.
Keep refrigerated.

SIDNEY WRITES...
Lovely!

My Mum's Chocolate Cake

Baroness Sarah Ludford MEP, London

INGREDIENTS:

6 oz self-raising flour
6 oz margarine or butter
6 oz caster sugar
3 eggs
2 level tbsp cocoa
2 tbls milk
1 tsp instant coffee dissolved
in the milk (optional)

Butter Icing
4 oz softened butter
6 oz icing sugar
1 dessertspoon cocoa
1 tsp instant coffee dissolved in
1 tbls milk

METHOD:

Pre-heat the oven to 160-170°C, 325°F, gas mark 3.
Line a 7" or 8" cake tin with greased paper.
Cream fat and sugar till fluffy.
Sift flour and cocoa together.
Beat eggs.
Stir spoonfuls of beaten egg and flour mixture alternately and gently into creamed fat and sugar.
Then add milk.
Put into tin and bake for 1¼ to 1½ hrs.
When cold, cut into 3 layers.

Topping

Beat together butter, icing sugar, cocoa and instant coffee dissolved in milk.

Cover top with icing made by melting 4 oz dark chocolate with 1-2 tsp hot water.

SARAH WRITES...

Comfort food extraordinaire! My favourite treat as a kid when my busy mother found time to bake. This is homely and easy to make chocolate cake, perfect on a Sunday afternoon with a cup of tea.

Plain Scones

Nick Harvey MP, Devon and Cornwall North

INGREDIENTS:

8 oz plain flour	2 oz butter or margarine
1 tsp cream of tartar	1 oz caster sugar
½ tsp baking soda	4 fl oz milk
Pinch of salt	Milk to glaze

METHOD:

Preheat oven to 220°C, 425°F, gas mark 7

Sift the flour, cream of tartar, baking soda and salt into a bowl.
Rub in the butter until the mixture resembles bread crumbs.
Stir in the sugar and enough milk to mix to a soft dough.
Turn on to a floured surface, knead and roll out to ¾ inch thickness.
Cut into 2 inch rounds and place on a floured baking sheet.
Brush with milk to glaze.
Bake for 10 minutes then cool on a wire rack.

Serve with lashings of Devonshire clotted cream, and home made strawberry jam and wash the lot down with a steaming mug of freshly brewed tea!

NICK WRITES...

I have chosen this simple recipe as I think there is nothing finer than spending a sunny Sunday in North Devon walking through the country lanes and stopping for afternoon tea in one of the delightful tea shops along the way. The debate over whether to apply liberal helpings of cream or jam first continues, I go for jam but feel very strongly that this is entirely a matter of personal taste.

Rock Cakes

Makes 16

Geoff Pope AM, Greater London Authority

INGREDIENTS:

A large flat, well greased
baking sheet
250gm plain flour
1 level tsp baking powder
75gm butter/margarine

75gm sugar
125gm raisins
¼ tsp nutmeg
1 egg
2 tbls milk

METHOD:

Preheat the oven to 200°C, 400°F, gas mark 6.

Sieve the flour and baking powder in a bowl.

Rub butter into the flour with the finger tips until the mixture is like fine breadcrumbs.

Stir in the nutmeg, sugar and raisins.

Beat the egg with the milk and add to the flour mixture.

Mix with a fork to a stiff mixture, not too sticky.

Divide the mixture into 16 and place on the baking tray.

Spike them with a fork to look like rocks.

Bake in a preheated oven for 10-15 minutes.

Cool on a wire tray.

Eat them immediately.

GEOFF WRITES...

A healthy, easy to make, tea-time treat. Great for picnics and the birds like the crumbs.

To be made by children for children. Granny or Granddad might need to help the little ones. If adults help they might be allowed to taste.

Yum...Yum...

Shortbread

Serves 4

Jo Swinson MP, Dunbartonshire East

INGREDIENTS:
225gm butter
110gm icing sugar
325gm plain flour
75gm corn flour

METHOD:
Preheat oven to 180°C, 350°F, gas mark 4.
Cream butter and icing sugar.
Add flour and corn flour.
Mix well and put on tray.
Bake for 1 hour.

JO WRITES...
This recipe is passed down from my grandfather who made shortbread his speciality. When he was selling his house in Renfrew to move to Milngavie, I remember, instead of a smell of bread, he used to bake his shortbread shortly before people arrived to view the property. I'm convinced it helped the house sale.

PARTY TIME

Aunt Mary's Chicken with Honey and Ginger

Sheila Rowell, Camden Liberal Democrats

INGREDIENTS:

6 joints of chicken	2 tsp candied peel
2 tbls oil	4-6 oz sliced mushrooms
Handful fresh mint (chopped)	Generous sprinkling of soya
2 tsp chopped rosemary	sauce
2 chopped cloves of garlic	1 tbls honey
1½ pieces root ginger	Salt and black pepper

METHOD:

Pre-heat the oven to 180°C, 350°F, gas mark 4

Fry chicken in oil till golden brown and place in large, shallow oven dish.

Sprinkle mint, rosemary, garlic, ginger, peel, salt and pepper over chicken.

Arrange mushrooms under and around.

Sprinkle oil, honey, and soy sauce over chicken.

Cover and cook for 75-90 minutes.

SHEILA WRITES...

In memory of my friend Mary Edmonds

Cassoulet

Baroness Sally Hamwee AM, Greater London Authority

INGREDIENTS:

1 lb haricot beans soaked
over night
1 large onion, peeled
2 cloves
Bouquet garni

½ lb streaky bacon, optional
½ lb garlic sausages or salami,
thick cut
3 lb chicken

METHOD:

In a large pan, put beans, onion stuck with cloves, and bouquet garni.
Cover with salted water, bring to simmer, cook gently for 1 hour.
Drain reserve liquor and onion.
Roast chicken, cool and lift off flesh in chunky pieces.
Finely dice bacon and sausage.
Combine beans, chopped up onion, bacon, sausage and chicken.
Add ½ pint bean liquor.
Cook gently in a slow oven for 1 hour, stirring occasionally.

SALLY WRITES...

The sort of thing to come back to after knocking on doors in the cold and
the wet. It stands cooking for a good deal longer if you get home later than
expected. Freezes well.

Dum Alu or Fried Potato Curry

Vincent Cable MP, Twickenham

INGREDIENTS:

1 lb potatoes (preferably walnut size)	1 tsp of ground coriander
1½ cups of cooking oil	6 cloves
¾ cup of grated onion	12 cardamom seeds
2½ tbls shortening	1 tsp salt
1 tbls poppy seed (roasted and ground optional)	½ tsp red chilli powder
1 tsp shredded green ginger root	½ tsp turmeric powder
6 cloves of garlic or 4 drops of garlic essence	¼ tsp ground pepper

METHOD:

Peel the potatoes and prick all over with a fork.

Keep dipped in salted water (about 1 tsp of salt) till all potatoes are peeled and pricked.

Remove potatoes from water and roll in a dry cloth to absorb the moisture.

Heat oil and fry the potatoes on medium heat until golden brown.

Remove from oil and keep for further use.

Heat fat in a saucepan and fry onions till crisp brown in colour.

Add all the spices, keep turning for 1 minute.

Combine onions, spices and potatoes.

VINCE WRITES...

My favourite is a simple vegetarian curry dish, often cooked by my late wife, Olympia. Olympia was a (Goan) Indian who specialised in hot tasty curries which were much loved — as she was — by our family. My three children developed a taste for spicy food before they discovered Western dishes and this is one of their favourites. Best served with another curry (chicken or chick peas), either basmati rice or an Indian bread (like paratha), and a light Indian beer.

Fruity Chicken with Squash

Kirsty Williams AM, Welsh Assembly Brecon and Radnorshire

INGREDIENTS:

    I tbls vegetable oil
    60 gm/2½ oz onion, peeled and chopped
    110 gm/4oz chicken breast, cut into chunks
    300 gm/10½ oz butternut squash, peeled, de-seeded and chopped
    300 ml/10fl oz unsalted chicken stock or water
    I small apple, peeled, cored and chopped

METHOD:

Heat the oil in a saucepan and sauté the onion until softened.
Add the chicken breast and sauté for 3-4 minutes.
Add the butternut squash.
Pour over the stock or water.
Cover and bring to the boil.
Then simmer for about 10 minutes.
Add the apple and cook until the chicken is cooked through and the butternut squash is tender, about 5 minutes.

Serve with rice, pasta or couscous.

KIRSTY WRITES...

I have to admit that cooking is not one of my strong points. Everything I do needs to be simple and quick. This is one of my children's favourites and ensures they get some fruit and vegetables. It can also be frozen, therefore handy when I get home after a late vote.

Ginger Nut and Chocolate Spread Pudding

Shirley Malin, Camden Liberal Democrat

INGREDIENTS:

I pkt of ginger nut biscuits
I jar of good quality chocolate spread
I carton whipping cream
Sherry, sweet or dry (according to taste)

METHOD:

Generously spread chocolate spread on both sides of biscuits and stick together (rather like a Swiss roll).

Put on an oval shape plate covered with foil.

Pour enough sherry over the biscuit roll till all the biscuits are well soaked, no longer dry but not soggy.

Leave in fridge for several hours.

Just before serving, whip cream to a piping consistency and spread over roll.

Decorate as you like.

SHIRLEY WRITES...

This 'party recipe' has been around a long time, but one of my favourites. Because it is extremely easy to do and very quick to prepare — and quite delicious (though not good if you are trying to lose weight).

Lemon and Ginger Cheesecake

Serves 12 and freezes well

Roger Hughes, Camden Liberal Democrat

INGREDIENTS:

> 250-300 gm ginger biscuits crumbs
> (ginger crunch are best, but ginger nuts will do)
> 800 gm soft cheese (fat content should be around 25%)
> 1 tsp vanilla essence
> 4 large or 5 medium eggs
> 250 gm granulated sugar
> Grated rind of one un-waxed lemon
> 1 tbls lemon juice (normally less that half the lemon)

METHOD:

Pre-heat the oven to 190C, 170C with fan, 375F, gas mark 5

Line a spring form pan (20cm for thick cake, 25cm for thinner) with aluminium foil.

Press the biscuits crumbs over the base. Put in fridge to chill.

Mash the cheese with the vanilla essence until soft.

Beat the eggs until thick and creamy then beat in the sugar gradually.

Continue beating while adding the cheese mixture in small portions, mixing each time until smooth.

Lastly, mix in the lemon rind and juice, making sure the lemon rind does not cling to the whisk.

Spread the mixture over the crumb base and bake for 25-30 minutes.

Allowing the cake to cool in the oven with the door open will reduce surface cracks.

Chill before removing from the tin.

Serve plain or with crème fraîche.

ROGER WRITES...

I developed this recipe myself about twenty years ago, trying to replicate the heavy, vanilla, New York style cheesecake I loved. This is not such a cheesecake. It is light and crumbly and very morish. So I stopped experimenting and settled for this instead. One day I will get round to developing a recipe for the New York style. I used to use digestive biscuits, but find ginger biscuits add a distinctive sweetness that offsets the lemon.

Mango and Bulgar Wheat Salad

Serves 4 as a side dish, 2 as a main course

Jo Shaw, PPC Holborn and St Pancras

INGREDIENTS:

100g bulgar wheat
1 large ripe mango
1 red onion
Bunch of fresh mint
2 tbls olive oil
Lemon / lime juice
Salt and fresh black pepper

METHOD:

Soak the bulgar wheat in cold water for about 15 minutes.
Peel the mango over a large bowl, making sure you catch all the juice.
Chop the flesh into bite sized pieces.
Chop the red onion and the mint and add to the mango pieces.
Drain the bulgar wheat and squeeze out remaining water with your hands,
then add to the mango, onion and mint.
Pour over the olive oil and lemon or lime juice. Add seasoning to taste.
Enjoy!

JO WRITES...

Quick, easy, healthy and delicious!

Mayoral Carbonara

Serves 4

Jill Fraser, London Borough of Camden Councillor and Mayor 2006/7

INGREDIENTS:

Spaghetti or any pasta of your choice
½ pound minimum bacon cut in approx ½ inch squares
1 onion finely chopped, optional
2 cloves garlic crushed
1 egg
8oz tub single cream or yoghurt if preferred
Approx 2 tbls parmesan cheese

METHOD:

Start cooking pasta.
Fry bacon and onion and garlic until well done and crisp.
Mix egg, cream and parmesan together.
Drain pasta and put back in saucepan over a low heat, and pour over cream mixture, stir well until cream sets.
If you want your pasta dry, cook a bit longer, or in sauce.
Do not cook for long, but keep stirring to required consistency.
Put on serving plate or individual bowls and sprinkle as little or as much bacon over the top to taste.

Serve with more parmesan and black pepper to taste.

JILL WRITES...

This recipe is very quick and incredibly flexible in the amount of bacon needed. My family love loads and this recipe works well with cheaper cuts and quality, including off-cuts, as well as expensive ones. I am not normally a cook who measures ingredients, so I hope these measurements work for you.

Minced Beef Stir Fry

Serves 4

Sharon Bowles MEP, South East England

INGREDIENTS:

> 500 gm minced or ground beef, ideally low fat (10% or 5%) and it is
> worth using organic or grass-fed beef for the flavour
> 500 gm mushrooms, sliced. Any will do, I use portabella flats
> 3 medium or 2 large onions, sliced or chopped, I keep them
> reasonably chunky and often put in some spring onions as well
> 2 sliced or coarsely chopped peppers, I usually use green and yellow

---

METHOD:

Put mince and onions in an open deep frying or sauté pan.
No extra fat is need but it does help to use a non-stick pan.
Stir so the mince is separated and mixed with the onion and cook for
about 5 minutes over a medium heat.
The higher the heat the more you have to stir, so I use a lower heat and
stir occasionally while I get on with chopping the mushrooms and peppers.
The mince will begin to look cooked, grey rather than brown, and the
onions will soften which is the key to when the next ingredients can be
added. If the mince is not low fat it may be possible to drain off surplus fat
at this stage. I then add the mushrooms, stir in and cook for another 2 or
3 minutes, followed by the peppers (and if using them spring onions) for
another 2 or 3 minutes.
Season with salt and a liberal amount of ground black pepper.

This dish can be eaten immediately or allowed to cool and reheated. It will
store in the refrigerator for several days. I enjoy it on its own, but I have
also combined it with cheesy dishes such as cauliflower cheese or with
cheesy potatoes (grate cheddar over steamed potato slices).

SHARON WRITES...

I like this recipe because it is quick. Also, if done in a larger quantity
reheats well with a zap in the microwave. In truth, almost everything could
be changed, ingredients and proportions. I like this particular combination
which I put together when I needed to eat more red meat (for iron)
and wanted to include more coloured vegetables in my diet for their
antioxidant value.

Quick Prawn Curry

Serves 3 to 4

Norman Lamb MP, North Norfolk

INGREDIENTS:

Large prawns
(peeled or defrosted)
2 onions
1 tbls olive oil
1 tbls plain flour
¼-½ pint chicken stock
2 tsp tomato puree

½-1 lemon (juice)
2 tbls mango chutney and plum
jam mixed
3-4 tbls of double cream or
yoghurt or coconut milk with
1tbls creamed coconut grated
Curry powder to taste

METHOD:

Peel and chop onion and fry until soft but not brown.

Stir in curry powder, fry briefly.

Stir in flour and fry for 2-3 minutes.

Add stock and stir well until the flour is well mixed in and the sauce much thicker.

Bring to boil and add tomato puree, chutney and lemon juice.

Simmer for a few moments.

Add prawns and heat through.

When you are ready to eat add double cream or other alternatives.

Serve with rice, green salad and maybe some torn coriander leaves.

Simple Tuna Fish Cakes

Serves 4

Lord Paddy Ashdown of Norton-sub-Hamdon GCMG KBE PC

INGREDIENTS:

3-4 medium potatoes
Salt and pepper
Knob of butter
1 egg
1 tin of tuna

2 heads of chopped parsley
Fresh brown breadcrumbs
(which give the fish cakes,
when fried, a crispy cover)
Oil

METHOD:

Cook the potatoes and mash well with salt, pepper and butter.
Add the beaten egg and tuna.
Mix well together and add the parsley.
Make cakes by taking a good handful of the mixture, roll in the
breadcrumbs and mould into flat cakes about ½ inch thick.
Fry on both sides for 2-3 minutes, and place on a baking tray in a moderate
oven for ½ an hour.

PADDY WRITES...

Delicious with baked tomatoes and peas. Kids love them.

Smoked Salmon Pasta

Serves 4

Michael Moore MP, Berwickshire Roxburgh and Selkirk

INGREDIENTS:

500 gm dried tube or shell
pasta
60 gm butter
1 medium onion, finely
chopped
500 ml crème fraîche

2 large handfuls fresh
mushrooms, peeled and
roughly chopped
400 gm smoked salmon, sliced
into bite size pieces
2 tbls Parmesan, freshly shaved
Freshly milled black pepper

METHOD:

Boil a large deep pan of water, add salt and some drops of olive oil.
Add the pasta, return to the boil and cook 8-10 minutes on a rapid boil
until the pasta is tender but firm.
Be careful not to overcook the pasta, it should be al dente.
Drain immediately.
Meanwhile, melt the butter in a medium saucepan, add the chopped onion
and cook gently on a medium heat for 6 minutes.
Add the mushrooms to the pan, stir and cook for a further 4 minutes on a
medium heat.
Return the drained pasta to its pan and stir in the crème fraîche.
Add the smoked salmon pieces, onions and the mushrooms.
Stir thoroughly and warm gently on the hob for a few minutes.
Add some freshly milled black pepper.
Spoon into the centre of pre-warmed pasta bowls, liberally sprinkle fresh
Parmesan shavings on top and serve.

MICHAEL MOORE WRITES...

I like this dish because it is simple and quick to make but, if done correctly,
tastes delicious. The largest salmon river in the United Kingdom, the Tweed,
runs through my constituency in the Scottish Borders. Try to avoid farmed
salmon in this dish.

Italy is one of my favourite countries and I just love Italian food ! Broccoli
can be used in place of mushrooms in this dish if, unlike me, you're fond of
the green stuff. Serve this dish in wide bowls with a leafy salad.

Spaghetti Bolognese

Serves 4

Chris Huhne MP, Eastleigh

INGREDIENTS:

1 onion (ideally a med-style
   red edged)
Olive oil
1 kg of lean minced beef
2 cloves of garlic
1 small tin of concentrated
   tomato puree

1 cube of beef stock
Salt, pepper, bay leaf and
   oregano
Spaghetti of your choice
Parmesan
A glass of red wine

METHOD:

Place the finely chopped onion in a lightly oiled pan big enough to handle the whole sauce. I recommend olive oil from Kalamata in the Peloponnese, where my mother-in-law comes from. (Which has nothing to do with the recommendation !)

Break up the lean beef mince with your fingers into the pan continuing to stir until all the mince has gone grey.

Peel the skin of the 2 garlic cloves and finely chop, add to the pan and stir.

Add the tin of concentrated tomato puree and stir.

At this point, add about half a jug of beef stock, salt, pepper and a bay leaf. Simmer gently for as long as you can.

Add the glass of red wine and simmer for a further 5 minutes.

Add 3 pinches of oregano 5 minutes before serving.

Bring a pan of water to the boil, add a splash of olive oil to help keep the spaghetti separate.

When cooked drain well and pour hot water over the spaghetti to rinse away residue and stop sticking. Mix with the bolognese sauce.

Some solid parmesan cheese that can be grated over the spaghetti bolognese is perfection. Repeat whenever a taste of Italian sunshine is required.

CHRIS WRITES...

This is the ideal warm-up after winter delivering or canvassing with lots of carbohydrates and protein.

Spinach and Potato Garlic Salad

Lynne Featherstone MP, Hornsey and Wood Green

INGREDIENTS:

1lbs (450gm) new potatoes
5 tbls mayonnaise
¼ pint (150gm) single cream
1 tbls lemon juice
1 tbls olive oil

2 large peeled garlic cloves
4oz (100gm) fresh spinach
leaves
Salt and black pepper

METHOD:

Cook the potatoes until just soft then drain and peel.
Blend in food processor the mayonnaise, cream, lemon juice, and oil.
Then add spinach leaves and garlic, blend until all ingredients are smooth.
Add salt and pepper to taste.
Pour over potatoes and mix in well.

Cover and leave in fridge until needed.

LYNNE WRITES...

Having only a tangential relationship with my kitchen or cooking, the need to find something totemic to produce for Lib Dem socials forced me into finding a 'signature' dish that everyone would think was wonderful but that only took me literally a few minutes to make (outside of boiling the potatoes!) This phenomenal tasting potato salad has become the talking point of many fund raising occasions.

Strawberry Mousse

Serves 4

Jonathan Fryer, London Liberal Democrat

INGREDIENTS:

    1 tin of strawberries including ½ of the juice from it
    1 block strawberry jelly
    ½ pint of double cream

METHOD:

Cut up and melt the jelly in a moderate amount of boiling water.
When this is liquid pour in the strawberries and the juice and stir.
Put in the fridge and allow it to three quarter set (but not solid).
Remove from the fridge and whip in the cream until it becomes fluffy.
Put back in the fridge to set.

It will be ready to eat in a couple of hours, and for some reason tastes even better the following day.

ANYTIME

A Delicious Pudding

Don Foster MP, Bath

INGREDIENTS:

    1 pot of plain yoghurt
    1 pot of double cream
    1 tbls of soft brown sugar

METHOD:

Mix together the yoghurt and the cream.
Pour the mixture into two large wine glasses.
Lightly sprinkle soft brown sugar on the top of each.
Place in the fridge at least an hour before serving.

Bombay Salad

Russell Eagling, London Borough of Camden Councillor

INGREDIENTS:
- 1 tin of corned beef
- 1 tin of pineapple pieces (7oz)
- 1 tbls sultanas
- 1 tbls of desiccated coconut
- 4 tbls of salad cream or mayonnaise
- 1 tsp of curry powder

METHOD:

Cut the corned beef into cubes and mix in all the other ingredients. Serve on a bed of lettuce or mixed leaves.

RUSSELL WRITES...

No salad table is complete without some retro 70s dish - and this is as retro as they come. Think prawn cocktail, coq-au-vin, black forest gateaux and fondue parties. Then don a kaftan and start whipping up some bombay salad. Best eaten whilst listening to Demis Roussos.

Boston Baked Beans

Baroness Emma Nicholson of Winterbourne MEP, South East

INGREDIENTS:

½ lb of haricot beans
1 onion finely chopped
1-2 tbls oil

2 tsp demerara sugar
2 rashers of bacon (chopped)
2 large tsp of black treacle
2 tsp mustard

METHOD:

Soak the haricot beans overnight and drain.
Cook in fresh water until tender.
Fry the finely chopped onion in oil until soft.
Add the rashers of chopped bacon and cook.
Next add the black treacle, the mustard and demerara sugar.
Mix and pour over baked beans and cook briefly.

EMMA WRITES...

This recipe has long been a favourite with my family - and is the real thing!
It is also a very simple and child-friendly dish.

Breakfast Banana Smoothie

Charles Kennedy MP, Ross Skye and Lochaber

INGREDIENTS:
    1 banana
    250ml milk
    3 tbls natural yoghurt
    1 tsp honey

METHOD:
Place all the ingredients in a blender and blend for 15 seconds.

CHARLES WRITES...
This makes a healthy frothy drink! It's a perfect way to start the day.

Drehniki a la Cormontoise

Serves 6

Charles Marquand, Camden Liberal Democrat

INGREDIENTS:

6 medium potatoes
(washed but not peeled)
1 small onion
2 eggs
3 tbls of flour

1 tsp salt
¼ tsp pepper
Several cloves of garlic to taste
Vegetable oil

METHOD:

Grate potatoes and onion, but not finely and squeeze well to remove as much liquid as possible.

Blend the grated potato and onion well.

Add the flour, lightly beaten eggs, salt, pepper and crushed garlic.

Heat oil (but not smoking) to cover bottom of large skillet.

Drop tbls of the mixture into the skillet and cook on both sides; squashing flat with a spatula.

When cooked drain well on paper towels.

To keep warm heat oven to 200°F, 100°C, gas mark 1

They are best eaten on a cold day. They go well with cold meats.

CHARLES WRITES...

This is a simple recipe for potato pancakes with a slight twist. It was given to me by Olga, a Russian who was staying with us in northern France in the village of Cormont. Olga lives in Tomsk, Siberia. She had been given this recipe by her grandmother who came from Belorussia. "Drehniki" is the Belorussian for potato pancakes. The "a la Cormontoise" refers to the addition of crushed garlic, a variation arrived at in Cormont. Extensive market research has shown that it is always wise to make significantly more pancakes than you think you might want — as a hard day in the Pripet marshes of Belorussia or in the Siberian forests or on the Channel beaches seems to stoke up an appetite.

Fairtrade Banana Fritters

Fiona Hall MEP, Northern England

INGREDIENTS:
300ml milk
100gm (4oz) plain flour plus a little extra for coating
25gm (1oz) caster sugar
2 tbls honey
4 bananas
Vegetable oil for deep frying

METHOD:
Mix the milk, flour, sugar and honey together.
Cut the bananas into four pieces.
Lightly flour each piece.
Dip them in the batter.
Deep fry in the oil for about 5 minutes until golden and crispy.
Drain well.

Serve the fritters on their own or with this delicious honey or chocolate sauce.
300 gm bitter dark chocolate, chopped
2 tbls of honey
150 gm butter
75 ml double cream

Mix all the ingredients in a bowl over simmering water until chocolate has melted.

Granola

Susan Kramer MP, Richmond Park

INGREDIENTS:

1½ lbs uncooked oatmeal   3fl oz honey
  or rolled oats   3fl oz light and tasteless oil
8 oz un-toasted wheat germ   1 tsp vanilla extract
2 tbls brown sugar   Seeds, nuts and dates to taste
3 tsp ground ginger

METHOD:
Combine in a pan all the dry ingredients except the seeds nuts and dates.
Combine honey, oil and vanilla and warm in microwave for 30 seconds.
Drizzle the warm liquid over the dry ingredients.
Microwave on a medium to high setting for 10 -15 minutes, stirring from
time to time.
Stop cooking when the oats are darkening nicely.
Add the seeds, nuts and dates.
Cool and scrape out the pan before it hardens too much.
Keep in an airtight container.

SUSAN WRITES...
I got fed up with paying high prices for breakfast cereals which you can
make easily at home. And with home preparation you can control the
ingredients. This Granola is a family favourite adapted from a couple of
recipes. My kids prefer a variation with cinnamon instead of ginger and no
dates but raisins and other dried fruit.

Liberal Porridge de Luxe

2 large servings, 3 moderate or 4 small

Robin Young, Camden Liberal Democrats

INGREDIENTS:

    1 English eating apple (Cox, Royal Gala, or similar)
    ½ lb raspberries
    3 tbls light runny honey, such as acacia, orange blossom or maple
      syrup if preferred
    1 cup traditional porridge oats
    3 equal cups of breakfast (Channel Island) milk (soya milk is also
      acceptable as an alternative)
    1 knob of unsalted butter
    1 sachet brown sugar (optional)
    Small tub of Cornish clotted cream
    More milk, honey, brown sugar, maple syrup, chopped dried fruit, or
      cream can be added to taste

METHOD:

Core, slice and dice the apple and microwave with a few drops of lemon
juice and 1 tbls of vanilla vodka for 1¾ minutes.

Mix raspberries with 3 tbls of honey of your choice or maple syrup, stand
until required.

Add oatmeal to pan, mix in milk stirring all the time, bring to the boil.

Add butter stirring all the time.

Cook over gentle heat for 15 minutes, stirring occasionally.

Take off heat and gently stir in the clotted cream.

Add the fruit mixture, again stirring in gently.

Serve the porridge into individual bowls to which optional additional
toppings may be added according to personal taste.

ROBIN WRITES...

Recommended preparation for delivering (or for recovery from delivering
of) Good Morning leaflets! My qualifications for offering a recipe, by
the way, include that I am a founder member of the British Academy of
Gastronomes! There are thousands of recipes for porridge making it more
tasty or sustaining. The one above is my personal favourite.

Luxury Red Cabbage

Lord Bill Rodgers of Quarry Bank

INGREDIENTS:

1 medium-sized red cabbage (about 1kg)	½ glass of claret (or any red wine)
1 big Bramley apple	3 dessert spoons of unrefined dark brown sugar
½ medium-sized onion	
70 to 80 gm sultanas	Goose fat
2 rashers of streaky bacon	Olive oil
1 tbls of wine vinegar	¼ cup of water

METHOD:

Cut the red cabbage into narrow strips and put in large aluminium pot, or comparable.

Peel and core the apple and cut into segments, adding to the cabbage.

Deal with the onion in a similar way.

Cut the bacon into 2 inch pieces and add to the pot together with the sultanas.

Add the wine, wine vinegar, water and a knob of goose fat.

Sprinkle over the sugar.

Put lid on the pot and simmer at a low heat for 2-2 ½ hours, stirring occasionally making sure it does not dry out.

Add a few dribbles of olive oil and the red cabbage is ready to serve. However, red cabbage is usually improved if it is allowed to cool, put in fridge for a day or so and then re-heated slowly.

BILL WRITES...

The origin of this recipe was in Lubartov, Poland, after which it passed by word of mouth through my wife's family to Berlin and then London. The recipe was much elaborated by Silvia and became immensely popular with our friends. This is the latest version and it has never been written down before.

Old Fashioned Concentrated Lemonade

Paul Burstow MP, Sutton and Cheam

INGREDIENTS:

3 lemons
1¾ lbs granulated sugar
¾ oz of citric acid
2 pints of cold water

METHOD:

Put 2 pints of cold water in a large saucepan.

Grate the zest of the 3 lemons into the water, add the sugar.

Put on a low heat and stir until all the sugar has dissolved.

Now gradually bring this to a slow simmer and continue to simmer for an hour.

Take off the heat, allow it to cool a little, and then pour the contents into a basin.

Stand overnight.

The next day, squeeze the juice of the 3 lemons and add to the liquid in the basin.

Dissolve the citric acid into a little of the liquid in a cup, using a wooden spoon. Then add to the liquid again. Stir well.

Pour it through a fine sieve to get rid of any pips.

Using a funnel pour into screw cap bottles and store in the fridge until needed.

PAUL WRITES...

This used to be made by my wife's grandmother Cecily Longbottom, it is delicious. Drink it either with water or with fizzy lemonade

Parsnip and Horseradish Mash

Bill Newton Dunn MEP, East Midlands

INGREDIENTS:
250gm parsnips after peeling
250gm floury potatoes after peeling
75ml of milk
50gm butter
Black pepper and salt
Horseradish finely grated

METHOD:
Cut the parsnips and potatoes into medium sized pieces and cook separately in salted water.
Scald the milk with the butter and mash with the cooked potatoes.
Add the cooked parsnip and mash again.
Add a grinding of black pepper and some finely grated horseradish.
Beat until the puree is creamy, light and fluffy.
Add extra horseradish, other seasoning and butter.
Reheat gently in a double boiler.

BILL WRITES...
Just right to serve with roast beef, beef stew, skewered and grilled lambs' kidneys, or sauté of chicken livers.

Question Time Late Night TV Snack

Lembit Opik MP, Montgomeryshire

INGREDIENTS:
¾ lb maturest cheese you can find
¼ pint milk
1 tbls flour
Mixed herbs
As much garlic sauce as you can stand

Cheese and chive crisps for dipping

METHOD:
Begin cooking at the start of the music and it should be ready by the end
of David Dimbleby's introductory comments.

Stir all the ingredients together over a gentle heat until melted. Eat.
Warning, it doesn't taste good cold!
Anything left over can be used as a putty substitute around your windows.

LEMBIT WRITES...
Here's a recipe for your book. It's an old student friend favourite of mine,
and, believe it or not, does actually taste good ! It also has the added
advantage of being very quick to cook, and can be made with ingredients
that almost everyone will have lying around somewhere. I hasten to add
that I can cook normal food too, though I have to admit it doesn't happen
that often !

Speggled Eggs

Serves 2

Elspeth Attwooll MEP, Scotland

INGREDIENTS:

Saucepan A	Saucepan B
1 small onion	4 eggs
4 medium tomatoes	½ oz/12 gm butter
2 rashers of bacon	2fl oz/75ml milk
A small amount of olive oil	Salt and pepper to taste
or butter for frying	
Salt and pepper to taste	

METHOD:

Saucepan A - Chop the onion quite small.

Cut the bacon into bite size pieces.

Skin and core tomatoes and cut into pieces.

Put the oil/butter into a saucepan and place over a gentle heat.

Add the onion and fry until translucent.

Add the bacon pieces and cook until just done.

Then put in the tomatoes, season and cook till disintegrated.

Keep warm while preparing saucepan B.

Saucepan B - Beat the eggs, milk and seasoning together in a bowl.

Pour into the saucepan, drop in the butter and place over a gentle heat.

Stir continuously until the eggs are just scrambled.

Put equal quantities from each saucepan side by side on a warmed plate and serve with crusty bread.

ELSPETH WRITES...

In the early 1960's David Steel, not then elected, was invited to talk to the Queen's College Dundee Liberal Club — of which Malcolm Bruce was then President — and for a meal in one of the students flats afterwards. We (well, I) managed to burn the soup, as one does. A liberal, no pun intended, helping of curry powder was put in to attempt to rescue the situation. David was reminiscing about the occasion at a dinner in honour of Malcolm a couple of years back. He made no mention of the soup. That means either it did not taste as awful as I thought or that he had diplomatically forgotten about that aspect of his visit.

Tian de Nice

Serves 4

Priscilla McBride, Camden Liberal Democrat

INGREDIENTS:
2 lbs of chard, kale or spinach (perhaps even spring greens, although
I have never used them)
Olive oil
Salt
Fresh bread crumbs wholemeal or white

METHOD:
Pre-heat oven to 220°C, 425°F, gas mark 7
Whatever you use, pick it over and weigh out a good 2 pounds for four
people.
Wash, then spin twice in a salad spinner, leaving just a little moisture on the
leaves.
Gather into a bundle and slice finely.
Fill an oiled roasting pan or heat-proof ceramic dish and salt very lightly
because the natural vegetable salts come out strongly.
Moisten with a little olive oil.
Cover with fresh white or wholemeal breadcrumbs soaked in olive oil to
give a more enticing appearance and a nice crunch.
Put in a very hot oven.
After 10 or 12 minutes lower temperature to 180°C, 350°F, gas mark 4 and
continue to cook for 45 to 50 minutes.
Keep an eye on the bread crumbs.

PRISCILLA WRITES...
This is a very simple, utterly delicious vegetable dish from the region
around Nice. There are as many recipes for Tian de Nice as there are cooks
in the South of France. It can be made with chard, kale or spinach.
If you use spinach, mature, robust leaves cook very well, but if there is only
baby spinach, don't bother to slice it.

Welsh Rarebit

Lord David Steel of Aikwood

INGREDIENTS:
> 4 oz well matured cheddar cheese
> I oz butter
> Half a wine glass of brown ale
> Salt and pepper
> A dash of mustard
> Hot buttered toast

METHOD:
Grate the cheese.
Put cheese into a bowl with the butter, ale and seasoning.
Set this in a pan of hot water over a gentle heat.
Stir until melted.
When smooth and creamy pour over the toast and serve at once.

LITERATI

Amblongus Pie

Amblongus Pie
by Edward Lear

To Make An Amblongus Pie

Take 4 pounds (say 4½ pounds) of fresh Amblongusses, and put them in a small pipkin.

Cover them with water and boil them for 8 hours incessantly, after which add 2 pints of new milk, and proceed to boil for 4 hours more.

When you have ascertained that the Amblongusses are quite soft, take them out and place them in a wide pan, taking care to shake them well previously.

Grate some nutmeg over the surface, and cover them carefully with powdered gingerbread, curry-powder, and a sufficient quantity of Cayenne pepper.

Remove the pan into the next room, and place it on the floor. Bring it back again, and let it simmer for three-quarters of an hour. Shake the pan violently till the Amblongusses have become a pale purple colour.

Then, having prepared a paste, insert the whole carefully, adding at the same time a small pigeon, 2 slices of beef, 4 cauliflowers, and any number of oysters.

Watch patiently till the crust begins to rise, add a pinch of salt from time to time.

Serve up in a clean dish, and throw the whole lot out of the window as fast as possible.

Sent in by Chris Naylor, London Borough of Camden Council Councillor

HOUSE OF LORDS

HOUSE OF COMMONS

THE SCOTTISH PARLIAMENT

THE WELSH ASSEMBLY

THE EUROPEAN PARLIAMENT

THE GREATER LONDON AUTHORITY

LONDON BOROUGH OF CAMDEN COUNCILLORS

MEMBERS AND SUPPORTERS